Fonts and Special Characters for Websites

Table of Contents

Dale Stubbart

Fonts and Special Characters for Websites

Dale Stubbart

Fonts and Special Characters for Websites

Introduction

If you want to use different fonts on your website, other than the defaults; if you want to use special characters on your website (ones other than those on your keyboard); then this is the book for you.

While this book is intended for those who maintain websites, you don't have to be a heavy-duty website programmer to use these features.

Knowledge of HTML and CSS is helpful. There is some Javascript and some VBA in the book, but it is limited to certain sections of the book, which can be skimmed or skipped.

Dale Stubbart

Fonts and Special Characters for Websites

Part 1 – Fonts

Chapter 1 – Font Lists

In CSS there are 5 default fonts styles or generic fonts – serif, sans-serif, monospace, cursive, and fantasy. Serif means the font has serifs or little tic marks, like this font. Sans-serif means without serifs, like this font. Monospace means each character takes the same amount of space, like this `font`. Cursive is sometimes called Handwriting or Script, like this *font* and this *font*. Fantasy fonts are for titles. These are usually very bold and larger, like this **font**.

Your html might look like:

```
<p class="serif">The quick brown fox</p>
```

Your css might look like:

```
.serif {
font-family: serif;
}
```

This would show "The quick brown fox" in a serif font.

The default fonts depend on your operating system. They are:

Serif – Times or Times New Roman
Sans-Serif – Arial or Helvetica
Monospace – Courier or Courier New

Dale Stubbart

Fonts and Special Characters for Websites

Cursive – Comic Sans MS
Fantasy – Impact

You should build a font list (also called a font stack), so that if somebody viewing your website doesn't have a specific font on their computer, their browser will use a different font in your list. The first available font in your font list (reading from left to right) is the one the user will see when they browse your website.

Note: if a user changes their stylesheet, they may not see your fonts. Also if they change their default fonts (fairly tricky and not recommended), they will only see your font if you don't use the generic names listed above.

If you don't want to figure out your own font lists, check out CSS Font Stack at http://www.cssfontstack.com/. They recommend CSS font settings for headers, paragraphs, and some other HTML elements.

They recommend specifying the font-family for

Times New Roman as: font-family: TimesNewRoman, 'Times New Roman', Times, Baskerville, Georgia, serif;

Arial as: font-family: Arial, 'Helvetica Neue', Helvetica, sans-serif;

Courier New as: font-family: 'Courier New', Courier, 'Lucida Sans Typewriter', 'Lucida Typewriter', monospace;

Comic Sans MS as: sorry, they do not give a recommendation for Comic Sans MS. Instead, they give a recommendation for Brush Script MT: `font-family: 'Brush Script MT', cursive;`

Impact as: font-family: Impact, Haettenschweiler, 'Franklin Gothic Bold', Charcoal, 'Helvetica Inserat',

Dale Stubbart

Fonts and Special Characters for Websites

'Bitstream Vera Sans Bold', 'Arial Black', 'sans serif'; Note: change 'sans serif' to fantasy, if you're using this for a fantasy font for titles and you want to use the default fantasy font if none of your other listed fonts is found.

Note how font-names with multiple words are inclosed in single quotes. You can also use double quotes. sans-serif can also be 'sans serif'.

I use the default serif font for the body of my web pages – that is, I don't specify anything.

For headings, I let it default to sans serif default font (not specifying it) or use `font-family: arial, helvetica, verdana, tahoma, sans-serif;`

To get a monospace font, I use the `<pre>` html tag. I could also use `<code>`, `<kbd>`, and `<samp>` tags.

If I want a cursive font, I use this font-list:

font-family: "Lucida Handwriting","Monotype Corsiva","Bradley Hand ITC","Brush Script MT", Arial, Helvetica, cursive;

I don't like the cursive default, so I include Arial and Helvetica before it. To make sure those two fonts slope, I include `font-style:italic;` which makes all those fonts slope, but I can live with that (the other fonts already slope some, specifying italic may make them slope more). If you don't want your font to slope so much, remove the italic part. Chances are high that most people will have one of the other fonts listed before Arial on their computer.

I don't use fantasy fonts. I rely on heading tags and/or `font-weight:bold` instead. I may also specify font-size to

Dale Stubbart

Fonts and Special Characters for Websites

make the font larger than the default to create more impact – which is what fantasy fonts do.

In my print stylesheet, I use the following lists. These lists are created so that fonts which take less space are found first. This can save paper and ink. Evergreen is a font which was provided free by GreenPrint which was designed to save ink. It is now available at a price from Fonts.com.

Serif: font-family: "Goudy Oldstyle", Garamond, "Baskerville Oldface", Baskerville, "Times New Roman", Times, serif;

Sans-serif: font-family: Evergreen, "Arial Narrow", Tahoma, "Trebuchet MS", "Gill Sans", "   Gill Sans MT", Arial, sans-serif;

Monospace as: font-family: 'Courier New', Courier, 'Lucida Sans Typewriter', 'Lucida Typewriter', monospace; Note: No change in order.

Cursive: font-family: Evergreen,"Bradley Hand ITC","Lucida Handwriting","Monotype Corsiva","Brush Script MT",cursive;

Fantasy as: font-family: Impact, Haettenschweiler, 'Franklin Gothic Bold', Charcoal, 'Helvetica Inserat', 'Bitstream Vera Sans Bold', 'Arial Black', fantasy; Note: No change in order, even though Haettenschweiler is skinnier than Impact, since it is much skinnier. And, again, I try to avoid using Fantasy fonts, especially for print as they often take more ink to print.

I also specify a smaller font-size – 88%.

Dale Stubbart

Fonts and Special Characters for Websites

Final note on font lists: Try to keep your font lists to 10 fonts or less to make sure they load quickly.

Fonts and Special Characters for Websites

Chapter 2 – Web-Safe Fonts

Web-safe fonts are fonts which most people have available on their computer.

If you don't like the fonts in the font lists above, you can find other web-safe fonts at http://www.cssfontstack.com/.

You should limit the number of fonts on your page – it will load faster, especially if you use other fonts as explained below, and it will look better.

Dale Stubbart

Fonts and Special Characters for Websites

Chapter 3 – Using other Fonts

So, you don't like any of these fonts and want to use a different font on your website. First, upgrade your website to HTML5, if you haven't already done so.

Second, there's a hard way and an easy way to add other fonts to your website. Both are called embedding fonts.

The easy way is to use Google Fonts at https://www.google.com/fonts.

If I want to use *Dancing Script* font, I can add this to my stylesheet:

@import url(http://fonts.googleapis.com/css?family=Dancing+Script);

Or I can add this to my html, which loads the font a little faster:

<link href='http://fonts.googleapis.com/css?family=Dancing+Script' rel='stylesheet' type='text/css'>

If I am just going to use this font for a phrase ("Fancy Font" in this example), I can include those characters as follows:

Dale Stubbart

Fonts and Special Characters for Websites

@import
url(http://fonts.googleapis.com/css?family=Dancing+Script
&text=
Fancy%20Font);
   This will speed up loading the font since it will only load those characters.

   Sooner or later you'll want more characters in your phrase or you'll want the normal version of the font so I suggest you just load the entire font. It won't take that long, especially not if you have modPageSpeed enabled (check with your website host). Just don't load too many fonts.

   Google Fonts makes the coding simple:
1) Find the font you want to use. Click "Add to Collection". Find the next font, click "Add to Collection". Etc.
2) At the bottom of the page (at Collection) on the right-hand side, click on "Use".
3) On the next page, check all the styles you want to use, check all the character sets you want to use, Click on Standard and copy the code to your webpage. Or click on @import and copy the code to your stylesheet.
4) Add the fonts to your font lists: font-family: "Dancing Script", "Lucida Handwriting","Monotype Corsiva","Bradley Hand ITC","Brush Script MT", Arial, Helvetica, cursive; Note: at this point, I can remove some of these other fonts from the list. I keep them there, since there may be a gap between Dancing Script being loaded

Dale Stubbart

Fonts and Special Characters for Websites

and my page displaying. The browser will use the next available font in my font-list until the font is loaded. This is not likely to ever happen. It is just a fail-safe.

The problem with Google Fonts is that they're strictly for use on the web. Google doesn't provide any means to download the font. That's where SkyFonts comes in. SkyFonts enables the download of fonts from Google Fonts and from other font libraries (Fonts.com, MyFonts, Monotype, and Linotype). Google Fonts are free, the others may not be. Just download Skyfonts from Skyfonts.com, following the instructions. Skyfonts constantly monitors the web for upgrades to your fonts. If you don't want it to do so, right-click on the SkyFonts icon in your system tray and choose settings. Uncheck, Start Skyfonts on Machine Startup. Then right-click the icon again and choose Quit Skyfonts.

If you have another font you really, really want to use there is a way to embed that font. Just make certain that the font can be legally used on your website (some free fonts are not free for use on commercial websites). This method of embedding is more difficult than using Google Fonts (unless that font library offers you a simple way).

First, upload the TTF, OTF, or WOFF version of your font to your website (any one of these versions will do). Make sure you have a license to do this or that the font is an open source font.

Then, add `@font-face` to your stylesheet. `@font-face` creates a new `font-family`.

Dale Stubbart

Fonts and Special Characters for Websites

```
@font-face {
    font-family: "Dancing Script";
    src: url(dancing_script_700.ttf);
}
```

And, use that style later in your stylesheet.
```
h1 {
    font-family: "Dancing Script";
}
```

Remember the path of urls in stylesheets are relative to the path of your stylesheet. The path is not relative to the path of your webpage, as it is in your HTML.

More fonts are available from Brick Fonts. If you want to use these fonts, go to http://brick.im/fonts/ and click on the GITHUB link.

Adobe provides fonts at https://edgewebfonts.adobe.com/fonts and at https://typekit.com/fonts. (Typekit is not free.) Go to EdgeWeb, Click on a font and choose "Select this font". Follow the instructions. These instructions only offer a javascript option (e.g. `<script src="//use.edgefonts.net/abel.js"></script>` for abel font) rather than `@import` or `link` option as with Google Fonts (though Google Fonts also offers a javascript option).

Font Squirrel offers free commercial fonts, plus an option for embedding these fonts, it calls the WebFont Kit. This option takes a few more steps. I consider it to be the hard

Dale Stubbart

Fonts and Special Characters for Websites

way, but not that hard. You have to download the font, then upload it to your website (they suggest in or near the folder the stylesheet is in). Their stylesheet `@font-face` follows. It contains references to other versions of the font (.eot, .svg) which are for older browsers.

```
@font-face{
    font-family: 'MyWebFont';
    src: url('WebFont.eot');
    src: url('WebFont.eot?iefix') format('eot'),
        url('WebFont.woff') format('woff'),
        url('WebFont.ttf') format('truetype'),
        url('WebFont.svg#webfont') format('svg');
}
```

.ttf, .otf, and .woff are supposed to work on all modern browsers. You can upload all these different font files, or you can just upload the .ttf, .otf, or .woff and specify more fonts in your file list for users with older browsers. Most browsers nag users to upgrade to the latest version or do so automatically, so I don't worry about really old browsers.

Even though loading fonts to your website via Google Fonts or other methods mentioned above won't take long. Using a font from your computer might. It is recommended that you gzip it first (I'll let you research how to do that).

If your website is taking too long to load your font (even Google Fonts), use `<link>` rather than `@import`, and place `<link>` directly after `<head>` in your HTML.

If it's still taking too long and you're only using a few characters from the font, use images of those characters or phrases. See Chapter 7 – Using Images for Characters in Part 2.

Dale Stubbart

Fonts and Special Characters for Websites

Remember when testing fonts, that if a font exists on your computer, the browser will use it. Try using an alternate name in @font-face for the font-family. For Google Fonts, try testing with one you haven't downloaded to your computer.

Dale Stubbart

Fonts and Special Characters for Websites

Part 2 – Special Characters

Chapter 1 – HTML Entities

If you want to use special characters (ones other than those found on your keyboard), the easiest way to do this is to use HTML Entities – shortcut names for these characters.

If you wanted to write "I don't like this sentence – it stinks." on your website, complete with fancy quotes, you'd write

“I don’t like this sentence. – it stinks. ”

Each HTML entity starts with & and ends with ;. “ is left-double-quote. ’ is right-single-quote. – is n-dash (which is shorter than an m-dash, but longer than a hyphen). ” is right-double-quote. ’ is right-single-quote.

Dale Stubbart

Fonts and Special Characters for Websites

Some commonly used HTML entities are:

  – Non-Breaking Space

< – Less than sign (<), > – Greater than sign (>)

& – &

Currency signs: ¢ – cent sign (¢), ¥ – ¥, £ – £, € – €

© – copyright (©), ® – registered trademark (®), &tm; – trademark (™)

Fancy quotes: “ – ("), ” – ("), ‘ – ('); ’ – (')

• – bullet (•), ° – degree (°), … – (…)

– –, — —

  – Non-Breaking Space

A non-breaking space is used in place of a space where you don't want the words on either side of the space to split across a line. A non-breaking space is also used when you want multiple spaces since all browsers interpret multiple contiguous spaces as one single space.

You can use five   for indentation. Though a clearer way may be to use the following HTML:

```
<p>This is the first sentence of this paragraph. Now I want a line break.<br />
<span class="indent"></span>This is the second line of the paragraph.<br />
<span class="indent"></span>This is the third line of the paragraph.
</p>
```

With CSS as follows:

```
p {
```

Dale Stubbart

Fonts and Special Characters for Websites

```
text-indent: 1em;
}
.indent {
padding-left: 1em;
}
```

<, >, and & are used for clarity since < and > are parts of HTML tags and & is part of an HTML Entity.

The others are hopefully self-explanatory.

HTML Entities come in two flavors – HTML4 and HTML5. HTML4 entities are available in all modern browsers. Not all HTML5 entities are available in all modern browsers. Some HTML5 entities require special fonts to display. To find out how to display HTML5 entities which require special fonts, see Chapter 3 – Unicode Characters.

All HTML4 Entities are listed here http://www.w3schools.com/charsets/ref_html_entities_4.asp. They can be expressed by name or in decimal or hex notation (Note hex notation can be upper or lower case). The names are easiest to remember and decipher.

HTML Entities are case sensitive – normally all lower case.

If all you're using HTML entities for are quotes, it can be quite tedious to type them all the time. One option is to copy the text to Word. In Word, change all double quotes

Dale Stubbart

Fonts and
Special Characters
for Websites

to double quotes (this makes them fancy quotes). Change all single quotes to single quotes. Then change all left double quotes to `&ldquo;`, etc. Then copy the text back to your website. Refer to Appendix A – Word to HTML VBA Macro for VBA code which converts text typed in Word to simple HTML.

Another option, instead of typing all those HTML entities, is to use a Javascript Library. See Chapter 4 – JQuery and Friends.

Dale Stubbart

Fonts and Special Characters for Websites

Chapter 2 – Combining Diacritical Marks (Accents)

Note: Not all diacritical marks are accents.

Note: Combining diacritical mark means the mark is combined with the letter, rather than following or preceding the letter.

Most combining diacritical marks can be handled via HTML Entities. For instance à can be written as `&agrave;` (letter followed by diacritical mark name). À is written as `&Agrave;`. Note the use of uppercase `A` rather than lowercase `a` in the HTML Entity name.

The combining diacritical mark names are

grave – accent grave (slanting down toward right)

acute – accent acute (slanting down toward left)

circ – accent circumflex (^)

tilde – ~

uml – diaresis (also called trema or umlaut) – two dots over the letter

ring – ring, looks like small o above letter

Elig – `&AElig;` or `&aelig;`. Elig combines A & E as Æ. Elig uses capital E. elig uses lowercase e. Lig stands for

Dale Stubbart

Fonts and Special Characters for Websites

ligature – something used for tying or binding things together.

cedil – cedilla – looks like comma under the letter

slash – slash through letter

Only the letters A, C, E, I, N, O, U, and Y (upper and lowercase letters) have HTML Entity names for those letters combined with diacritical marks. Not all of those letters can be followed by all of the combining diacritical mark names.

Only the following HTML Entity names using combining diacritical marks exist:

&Agrave, &Aacute, &Acirc, &Atilde, Ä Å Æ

Ç

È É Ê Ë

Ì Í Î Ï

Ñ

&Ograve, &Oacute, &Ocirc, &Otilde, Ö Ø

Ù Ú Û Ü

Ý

&agrave, &aacute, &acirc, &atilde, ä å æ

ç

è é ê ë

ì í î ï

ñ

&ograve, &oacute, &ocirc, &otilde, ö ø

ù ú û ü

ý ÿ

Dale Stubbart

Fonts and Special Characters for Websites

Note: There is no `&Yuml;` `&Aelig;` or `$aElig;`

You may need to make other diacritical mark combinations, such as for phonetics or Pīnyīn (romanized/latinized/westernized Mandarin). To do this, you'll need to write the letter followed by a hex or decimal notation for the combining diacritical mark (there are no named equivalents for doing this). I'll list the hex notation. You can look up the decimal notation if you're so inclined.

The hexadecimal characters `&#x300;` through `&#x36F;` are used to combine diacritical marks with the preceding character - see https://en.wikipedia.org/wiki/Combining_Diacritical_Marks. The more common ones are:

`&#x300;` − grave; `&#x301;` − acute; `&#x302;` − circumflex; `&#x303;` − tilde; `&#x304;` − macron; `&#x305;` − overline; and `&#x30A;` − ring.

Examples of those:

à – grave; á – acute; – â – circumflex; ã – tilde; ā – macron; a̅ – overline; å – ring

There are stroke overlays which are better written as `<s>a</s>`, `<del>a</del>`, or `<span class="strikethrough">a</span>` where `.strikethrough` in stylesheet is

.strikethrough {
text-decoration: line-through;
}

text-decoration can be overline, line-through, or underline.

Dale Stubbart

Fonts and Special Characters for Websites

Combining diacritical marks can be combined by following one with another. For instance `u&#x308;&#x301;` displays the Pīnyīn letter ǘ.

You may need to separate successive combining diacritical marks or specify a diacritical mark by itself. Use the combining grapheme joiner (which doesn't join) `&#x34F;`, if no other way exists to separate them.

Dale Stubbart

Fonts and Special Characters for Websites

Chapter 3 – Unicode Characters

The easiest and fastest way to display special characters other than HTML4 Entities and Combining Diacritical Marks may be to use images. See Chapter 7 – Using Images for Characters. I've placed that chapter later because I think you should consider other options before making a decision as to which option to use.

Any character you want to display is a Unicode character. Keyboard characters, HTML4 Entities, and HTML5 Entities are Unicode characters. Every Unicode character can be referenced by a hex or decimal number. (I'll let you figure out the decimal or look it up, if you want to use it.) Hex for smiley face (☺) is `&#x263A;`. However, if it's a keyboard character, it's simplest to just type it from the keyboard. If it's an HTML4 Entity, it's simplest to reference it by its HTML4 Entity Name.

HTML5 Entities are listed here: http://dev.w3.org/html5/html-author/charref. HTML5 Entities include all the HTML4 Entities. HTML5 Entities can be referenced by name. There are about 200 HTML4

Dale Stubbart

Fonts and Special Characters for Websites

Entities. There are over 1500 HTML5 Entities, some of which can be referenced by more than one name. I would suggest using the hex value for HTML5 Entities since there are a lot of them and they don't always display correctly – it may remind you to double check to make sure it does display correctly and that you may have to use a different font to get it to display correctly.

Not all Unicode characters are displayable or display correctly unless you have the correct set of fonts and some of those fonts are only available for Apple/MAC computers. Keyboard characters and HTML4 Entities will display correctly. There is more on how to make Unicode characters display correctly later in this chapter.

Unicode characters include characters in almost all languages including English, Alphanumeric symbols, Numbers, Math symbols, Technical symbols, Punctuation, Braille, Music symbols, Dingbats (Wingdings), Emoticons, Transportation and Map Symbols, Game symbols, and other symbols.

If you're not interested in languages other than English, there are about 6500 Unicode Symbols you might be interested in using on your website. Finding the symbol you're looking for can be a simple matter of searching for it. For instance, searching for Unicode smiley face, will soon let you know that you can use `&#x263A;` to produce ☺.

Unicode characters are grouped into Unicode Blocks. Most, but not all of the Unicode characters in the following

Dale Stubbart

Fonts and Special Characters for Websites

Unicode Blocks are available for common fonts (which includes the web-safe fonts): Basic Latin, Latin-1 Supplement, Latin Extended-A, Latin Extended-B, IPA Extensions, Phonetic Extensions, Phonetic Extensions Supplement, Latin Extended Additional, Letterlike Symbols, Number Forms, Enclosed Alphanumerics, Latin Extended-C, Old Italic, Gothic, Mathematical Alphanumeric Symbols, Greek, Greek Extended, Ogham, General Punctuation, Currency Symbols, Number Forms; Math Operators, Geometric Shapes, Misc Math Symbols-A, Misc Math Symbols-B, Supplemental Math Operators, Arrows, Supplemental Arrows-A, Supplemental Arrows-B, Misc Symbols and Arrows, Misc Technical, Optical Char Recognition, Misc Symbols, Box Drawing, Block Elements, Ideograph Description Chars, Tai Xuan Jing Symbols, Misc Symbols, Dingbats, Misc Symbols and Pictographs, Emoticons, Transport & Map Symbols, and Braille. This limits you to about 5000 symbols.

If you want to use a Unicode symbol and want to make sure it will show up on most peoples' computers, test to see if it displays using Arial or Times New Roman font in Microsoft Word. In Microsoft Word, type the code (263A for Smiley Face), then press Alt+X – the result is ☺.

If you still can't see the character, add Symbola Font from http://zhm.github.io/symbola/. To find a list of fonts for each Unicode Block, go to FileFormat at http://www.fileformat.info/info/unicode/block/index.htm. Click on the "Unicode Block" which contains the Unicode Symbol you want to use. Then click on "Fonts that support

Dale Stubbart

Fonts and Special Characters for Websites

this block". Symbola covers most characters. LastResort appears to cover all characters. However, LastResort is only available on Apple Computers.

Note: The character presented by Symbola may be different from that presented by Arial or Segoe UI Symbol. Often the symbol you see when searching for Unicode symbols on the web is the one presented by Symbola.

See Chapter 7 – Using Images for Characters for an alternate method of displaying Unicode characters.

Dale Stubbart

Fonts and Special Characters for Websites

Chapter 4 – JQuery and Friends

Another method of creating fancy quotes is to use JQuery which is a javascript library found at https://jquery.com/. JQuery is a large javascript library (use the latest version for faster loading). Smaller libraries just for quotes include jsprettify at https://code.google.com/p/jsprettify/ and smartquotes.js at http://smartquotesjs.com/. (Smaller libraries should load faster.) For JQuery code, see https://gist.github.com/karbassi/6216412. Note, use

```
<script src="http://code.jquery.com/jquery-2.1.4.min.js"></script>
```
rather than
```
<script src="//ajax.googleapis.com/ajax/libs/jquery/1.10.2/jquery.min.js"></script>.
```

This blog from Dr Drang http://leancrew.com/all-this/2010/11/smart-quotes-in-javascript/ gives us this simple javascript function, which you have to call and work into your website.

```
// Change straight quotes to curly and double hyphens to em-dashes.
function smarten(a) {
    a = a.replace(/(^|[-\u2014\s(\["])'/g, "$1\u2018");     // opening singles
```

Dale Stubbart

Fonts and Special Characters for Websites

```
    a = a.replace(/'/g, "\u2019");                    // closing
singles & apostrophes
    a = a.replace(/(^|[-\u2014/\[(\u2018\s])'/g, "$1\u201c");
// opening doubles
    a = a.replace(/"/g, "\u201d");                    // closing
doubles
    a = a.replace(/--/g, "\u2014");                   // em-
dashes
    return a
  };
```

Another method is to use and style the `<blockquote>` or `<q>` tags. But getting that to work properly, and remembering to use those tags can be more headache than it's worth. The CSS would look like

```
blockquote, q {
    quotes: "\201C" "\201D" "\2018" "\2019";
}
```

Also, you may not want to override blockquote and q defaults, since sometimes browsers display these quotes differently, depending on the language of the user.

If you just want fancy quotes, HTML Entities may be the simplest way to go.

Use the smallest javascript library possible for the fastest load time.

Dale Stubbart

Fonts and Special Characters for Websites

Chapter 5 – CSS Libraries

If you want to use other symbols on your website, you can try to use the CSS Libraries FontIcons at https://fonticons.com/ (mostly paid versions) or the previous version FontAwesome at http://fortawesome.github.io/Font-Awesome/ (free).

To use FontAwesome, include this line at the top of your `<head>` section in HTML.
   <link rel="stylesheet" href="https://maxcdn.bootstrapcdn.com/font-awesome/4.4.0/css/font-awesome.min.css">
Then include this code in your HTML to display a smiley face:
   <i class="fa fa-smile-o"></i>
You can use `<span>` tags rather than `<i>` tags. They suggest using `<i>` tags because they're shorter and therefore easier to type. I prefer using `<span>` tags because I don't end up thinking that the icon is going to be italicized.
   FontAwesome currently has 585 icons.

Dale Stubbart

Fonts and Special Characters for Websites

Chapter 6 – Emoji

Emoji are images based on Japanese emoticons. Japanese emoticons incorporate several symbols, rather than the two or three in English emoticons. Japanese emoticons also don't require you to turn the screen or your head on its side to see what the emoticon is supposed to look like. Emoji are enabled on some smart phones by use of Emoji Short Codes. For instance a Grinning Face (☺) is `:grinning:`. See http://www.emoji-cheat-sheet.com/ for the complete list of symbols and shortcodes. Some Emoji display differently depending on the app.

While a smartphone or Facebook may interpret an Emoji shortcode and display the Emoji image, your website will not do so; not without some help.

If you want to use Emoji, try one of these Emoji Javascript Libraries - Emoji One at http://emojione.com/developers and http://git.emojione.com/demos/1.5.0/#js for demos, or Twemoji (Twitter Emoji) at https://github.com/twitter/twemoji and http://blog.farrant.me/adding-emoji-support-to-any-website/ for demos. Emoji One is the simpler one to use.

Dale Stubbart

Fonts and Special Characters for Websites

Using Emoji One, add these lines to your `<head>` HTML.
```
<script src="//cdn.jsdelivr.net/emojione/1.5.0/lib/js/emojione.min.js"></script>
<link rel="stylesheet" href="//cdn.jsdelivr.net/emojione/1.5.0/assets/css/emojione.min.css" />
```

Call the emojione.shortnameToImage javascript function, passing the Emoji shortcode (`:grinning:` for example):
```
<script>document.write(emojione.shortnameToImage(":grinning:"))</script>
```

If you're just using a few Emoji Characters, see Chapter 7 – Using Images for Characters.

Dale Stubbart

Fonts and Special Characters for Websites

Chapter 7 – Using Images for Characters

If you want to use a non-keyboard character on your website, find an image of that character and use it instead. This method is always reliable and will always work.

For images to work on the web, they should be in JPG, GIF, or PNG formats. Images should be compressed. They should also have a resolution of 72 pixels/inch. Compression and lower resolution will result in faster load times for the image. Different people have different opinions on the best image size. If the image will be a fixed size on the screen, I save the image at that size. Larger images will need to be resized for smaller screens. I find a maximum size of 3x4 inches (216x288 pixels) works well for most situations. Facebook prefers 400x400 pixels. Twitter prefers 120x120 pixels. Facebook and Twitter both prefer square images in their posts.

JPG presents the clearest image. GIF images have a smaller file size, but are limited to 256 colors as opposed to the more than 16 million colors for JPG. GIF can set one color to be interpreted as transparent. PNG may have

Dale Stubbart

Fonts and Special Characters for Websites

smaller file size then GIF. PNG have 16 million colors and 8 colors which can be interpreted as transparent.

GIF can be animated with Javascript.

For Unicode Characters, make sure you have the proper font downloaded. See Chapter 3 – Unicode Characters.

In Microsoft Word, type the code (263A for Smiley Face), then press Alt+X – the result is ☺. Change the font-size to 36 or larger (The image will scale down better than it will scale up). You can then copy the Smiley Face directly into Microsoft Paint into a Text Box (make sure to click outside the textbox when you're done with the text box).

Copy that image to another image editor – one in which you can set the transparent mask for gifs. Set the image size to 100x100 pixels or smaller. Save the image as a .gif. You want a transparent gif so that the image blends well with your website no matter what your background color. You may have to change the color of the image if you have a dark background. You may want to create one image with a dark color or black, and another image with the color inverted (light or white).

If you have an image editor which will do all these steps, use it instead.

In your HTML, use this code:

```
<img class="img_char" src="menu/char_smiley_face.gif" alt="Smiley" title="Ha!"/>
```

Create these classes in your stylesheet:

```
.img_char {
```

Dale Stubbart

Fonts and Special Characters for Websites

```
height:1em;
}
.img_char_x_large {
height:1.25em;
}
.img_char_xx_large {
height:1.5em;
}
.img_char_xxx_large {
height:1.75em;
}
.img_char_xxxx_large {
height:2em;
}
```

This CSS will help resize your images to the proper height, depending on the height of the line or the desired height of the image. I did not find it helpful to state the height more precisely than to the nearest .25 em.

For Emoji, copy the symbol from the Emoji Cheat Sheet at http://classic.getemoji.com/. Follow the instructions above for using images for Unicode Characters. Since different apps (think Android phone vs Apple phone) may display Emojis differently, you may want to copy your image from https://www.emojibase.com/. Click on the Emoji you want.

For example :grinning: shows the following variations: 😀 😃 😄 😁. The last three faces are orange, but this is a black and white book, so they're shown in grey-scale.

Dale Stubbart

Fonts and Special Characters for Websites

A third option is to copy an image from a clipart library. Go to https://openclipart.org/search/?query=icon+set to search for Icon Sets on OpenClipArt (free). For example, choose https://openclipart.org/detail/17694/15-small-smilies for 15 small smiley icons to use this smiley ☺ (converted from yellow to gray-scale). Other free clipart libraries include http://www.wpclipart.com/, http://www.freepik.com/, http://clipart.co, http://www.freepik.com/, and http://iconmonstr.com/. Clipart is usually a drawing rather than a photo.

A fourth option for finding images to use is to search an image or photo library. Here are some image libraries that are free and royalty free (you don't have to pay to use it on your commercial site). Remember, terms can change, so double check them before grabbing an image. http://www.freeimages.com/, https://pixabay.com/, http://www.morguefile.com/, https://freerangestock.com/, http://www.rgbstock.com/, http://www.dreamstime.com/free-photos, http://nos.twnsnd.co/. Images from image libraries may contain two much detail to work well when resized to character-height.

Remember to add the `alt=` property to your `<img>` tag. This enables screen readers (used by the visually impaired, aural learners, and others) to tell what your image is. If there is no `alt=` property, the reader may say "graphic" or the name of the image file. You can also add a `title=` property to your `<img>` tag if you want some text to pop up when the user hovers over the image. You can make the

Dale Stubbart

Fonts and Special Characters for Websites

alt= and/or title= properties say something other than stating what the object is, such as "Ha!" or "lol" rather than "Smiley".

  <img class="img_char" src="menu/char_smiley_face.gif" alt="Smiley" title="Ha!"/>

Dale Stubbart

Fonts and Special Characters for Websites

Chapter 8 – HTML5 Canvas 2-D

HTML5, now widely available on most browsers, provides the `<canvas>` tag for drawing 2-D (2-Dimensional) objects.

```
<canvas id="mydrawing" width="300" height="200"></canvas>
```

Back to HTML5 Canvas.

The canvas tag needs three attributes – ID, Width, and Height. You can give it a border via CSS.

The canvas tag does nothing by itself. Javascript uses the canvas ID to manipulate the canvas so that it ends up being a drawing.

You can use Javascript to draw shapes on the canvas, place images on the canvas, draw text on the canvas, or do any combination of those things. You can combine drawings, give your drawings transparency, use gradients, animate your drawings, add shadows, make your text look like outline text, give your text depth, etc.

Basic javascript for a canvas tag with id of mydrawing is

```
<script>
var canvas = document.getElementById('mydrawing');
var context = canvas.getContext('2d');
```

Dale Stubbart

Fonts and Special Characters for Websites

```
    // do something with the context
</script>
```

1) First, get the canvas element via the id – getElementById.
2) Second, get the context of the canvas – getContext. 2d says, use the 2-dimensional context. See Chapter 10 – HTML5 Canvas 3-D for 3-dimensional.
3) Then do something with the context.
   a) Set the starting point or origin of the drawing by context.moveTo(x,y), context.fillText('Hello World!', x, y), context.strokeText('Hello World!', x, y), context.drawImage(imageObj, x, y, width, height), or a similar method which specifies the origin. The x, y coordinates of 0,0 specify the top-left corner of the canvas. 0,width specify the top-right corner. 0,height specify the bottom-left corner. width,height specify the bottom-right corner.
   b) Connect points with lines or arcs using any of several statements. `context.lineTo(300,150);`, etc.
   c) Manipulate the drawing, adding more lines or segments, filling the drawing with a color, adding transformations etc.
   d) Finalize this part of your drawing, via stroke, fill, filltext, drawimage, stroketext, wraptext, or similar method. Note: Sometimes setting the origin, manipulating the drawing, and finalizing the drawing is all done by finalizing the drawing.
4) Finish your drawing by repeating steps 3 as needed to draw multiple objects on the canvas.

Dale Stubbart

Fonts and Special Characters for Websites

To clear the canvas to start over or during an animation, use:

context.clearRect(0, 0, canvas.width, canvas.height);

Animation consists of changing the x,y coordinates every so often over time. You could also animate varying other aspects of the drawing such as width, height, color, text.

The best tutorial for working with the HTML5 canvas is the HTML5 Canvas Tutorial by Eric Rodwell at http://www.html5canvastutorials.com/advanced/html5-canvas-linear-motion-animation/ with accompanying reference page at http://cheatsheetworld.com/programming/html5-canvas-cheat-sheet/.

W3 Schools offers their overview pages at http://www.w3schools.com/html/html5_canvas.asp and http://www.w3schools.com/tags/ref_canvas.asp.

DiveIntoHTML offers this tutorial http://diveintohtml5.info/canvas.html. It suggests resetting the canvas by setting `canvas.width=canvas.width`. However, `context.clearRect` mentioned above is the preferred method, meaning it clears the canvas better. This tutorial also explains how to make sure your lines fit inside your canvas, by taking into consideration the line width and height.

Dale Stubbart

Fonts and Special Characters for Websites

Chapter 9 – HTML5 Canvas 2-D using jsDraw2DX

Drawing images with HTML5 Canvas, requires knowing some trigonometry. The more complex the image, the more trigonometry is required. Drawing simple squares, adding rounded corners, adding text, coloring the text are all fairly simple. Drawing lines that are not horizontal or vertical and drawing curves (other than rounded corners on squares) can quickly get complex. You pass parameters to javascript functions to draw the object on the canvas. The parameters are in coordinates (from the top-left corner, rather than bottom-left or center-center), and in radians (rather than degrees).

Luckily, there is help in the form of Javascript Libraries. Most of the libraries only simplify the number of steps and perhaps combine parameters. Or they use a different syntax which doesn't simplify much. They typically don't simplify the trigonometry although some claim to by using vector math instead. jsDraw2DX from jsFiction simplifies the trigonometry and the number of parameters. Basically you tell it where you want to start drawing, what you want to draw (rectangle, lines, circle, curve, etc), and the size of

Dale Stubbart

Fonts and Special Characters for Websites

what you want to draw. It figures out the rest. It still keeps functions for the more complex curves like Bezier, but also adds a simple drawCurve function. You simply pass points you want to be included in the curve to drawCurve.

For jsDraw2DX, include the following in your `<head>` tag:

```
<script type="text/JavaScript"
src="jsDraw2D.js"></script>
```

Basic javascript for a canvas tag with id of mydrawing using jsDraw2DX is

```
<script>
var canvas = document.getElementById('mydrawing');
var graphic = new jsGraphics(canvas);
// do something with the graphic
</script>
```

Dale Stubbart

Fonts and Special Characters for Websites

1) First, get the canvas element via the id – getElementById.
2) Second, create a jsGraphics Object.
3) Then do something with the context.
   a) Create a pen specifying color and width `var pen = new jsPen("red",1).`
   b) Define points `var pt1 = new jsPoint(20,30);.` The x, y coordinates of 0,0 specify the center-center of the canvas.
   c) Draw the line or arc through the points using any of several statements.
      `graphic.drawLine(pen,pt1,pt2);,` etc.
   d) Manipulate the drawing, adding more lines or segments, filling the drawing with a color, adding transformations etc.
   e) Finalize this part of your drawing with fill, text, etc.
4) Finish your drawing by repeating step 3 as needed to draw multiple drawings on the canvas.

To clear the canvas to start over or during an animation, use: `graphic.clear();.`

jsDraw2DX is only for drawing, not for animation. See Chapter 8 – HTML5 Canvas 2-D to get ideas on how to manipulate the drawing using javascript.

Dale Stubbart

Fonts and Special Characters for Websites

Chapter 10 – HTML5 Canvas 3-D

Once you've got a good handle on using canvas to draw 2-dimensional drawings, you can try your hand at 3-dimensional canvas drawings.

To draw 3-dimensional canvas objects, your basic javascript would look like this:

```
<script>
var canvas = document.getElementById('mydrawing');
var context = canvas.getContext('webgl');
// do something with the context
</script>
```

Notice the context is webgl rather than 3d. webgl is based on OpenGL which is an API for drawing 2-dimensional and 3-dimensional objects. More info on OpenGL is available from the Krhonos group at https://www.khronos.org/opengl/. If you have questions about webgl which the webgl references below don't answer, try using the Krhonos OpenGL reference to answer them.

After setting the context, you create a drawing buffer which contains a color, depth, and a stencil buffer. The

Dale Stubbart

Fonts and Special Characters for Websites

depth buffer controls the third dimension. The stencil buffer controls which fragments of the image are drawn and which aren't.

If you resize the canvas (change width or height), set the viewport as follows:

mydrawing.viewport(0, 0, mydrawing.drawingBufferWidth, mydrawing.drawingBufferHeight);

HTML5 Rocks as a webgl Tutorial at http://www.html5rocks.com/en/tutorials/webgl/webgl_fundamentals/. This tutorial assumes you know what you're doing, but is still a good reference.

If you're going to use webgl, you might want to use the Pixi.js javascript library http://www.pixijs.com/.

Dale Stubbart

Fonts and Special Characters for Websites

More information on webgl is at https://www.khronos.org/webgl/wiki/Main_Page. Reference starts on that page at DOM Interfaces https://www.khronos.org/registry/webgl/specs/1.0/#5.

I'll let you figure out the rest.

Dale Stubbart

Fonts and Special Characters for Websites

Chapter 11 – SVG

An alternative to using the HTML5 Canvas is to use an SVG image. SVG is good to use if you are drawing fewer than 15 objects. Otherwise, it can take too much memory and it will be better to use HTML5 Canvas. Also, HTML5 Canvas is the current standard, though SVG is probably not going away any time soon. An SVG image is a set of XML statements which create the drawing. These XML statements are similar to the HTML5 Canvas Javascript statements. SVG images can be styled with CSS, but use different CSS statements than regular images http://www.w3.org/TR/SVG/styling.html. SVG images can be animated via the `<animate>` SVG XML statement.

You can display an SVG image on you website by specifying the image via an `<img>` or `<object>` tag, or by placing the `<svg>` portion of the XML in the SVG image into the HTML code.

Specify the image via an `<img>` tag as follows: `<img src="image.svg" />`.

Specify the image via an `<object>` tag as follows: `<object type="image/svg+xml" data="image.svg"><object>`

Dale Stubbart

Fonts and Special Characters for Websites

The <SVG> tag will look something like this:

```
<svg id="svgimage" width="21cm" height="13.5cm"
viewBox="0 0 210 135"></svg>
```

If your SVG code is as follows:

```
<svg id="svgimage" width="21cm" height="13.5cm"
viewBox="0 0 210 135">
 <rect x="10" y="20" width="150" height="70"
fill="#eeeeff" stroke="red" stroke-width="1" />
 </svg>
```

and you want to use this code as a separate SVG Image file, it needs to be changed to look like the code at the top of the next page.

Dale Stubbart

Fonts and Special Characters for Websites

```
<?xml version="1.0" encoding="UTF-8"
standalone="no"?>
<!DOCTYPE svg PUBLIC "-//W3C//DTD SVG 20010904//EN"
  "http://www.w3.org/TR/2001/REC-SVG-
20010904/DTD/svg10.dtd">
<svg version="1.0"
xmlns="http://www.w3.org/2000/svg" width="21cm"
height="13.5cm" viewBox="0 0 210 135"
preserveAspectRatio="xMidYMid meet">
  <rect x="10" y="20" width="150" height="70"
fill="#eeeeff" stroke="red" stroke-width="1" />
</svg>
```

That is, the <?xml> tag and the <!DOCTYPE svg> tags must be added. Also the <svg> tag will also need the xmlns= attribute. The version= and preserveAspectRatio= attributes are helpful, but optional.

The x, y coordinates of 0,0 specify the top-left corner of the canvas. 0,width specify the top-right corner. You can specify a new 0,0 coordinate offset from the original 0,0 coordinate.

You pass all the parameters to the function of what you want to draw. Lines requires the coordinates of both points. Rectangles require the starting point, width, and length. Arcs require the control points and are normally drawn using the path function.

You can convert an image to an SVG image so you can style it more with CSS by converting it with an online converter (MobileFish at http://www.mobilefish.com/services/image2svg/image2svg .php, PicSVG at http://picsvg.com/, or Autotracer at

Dale Stubbart

Fonts and Special Characters for Websites

http://www.autotracer.org/. You may lose some definition since these programs trace the picture to convert it to SVG.

An SVG tutorial is available at http://www.w3schools.com/svg/default.asp. Use the links on the left to see the various drawing statements. Another tutorial is at http://tutorials.jenkov.com/svg/index.html. It explains the path statement in more detail.

SVG is normally used for 2-dimensional drawings. More definition can be added to the drawings to make them look 3-dimensional. The recommended approach is to use HTML5 Canvas webgl. See Chapter 10 – HTML5 Canvas 3-D.

To convert your SVG images to HTML5 Canvas, try one of these online converters: http://www.professorcloud.com/svg-to-canvas/ or http://demo.qunee.com/svg2canvas/.

They both use the Canvg javascript library. You can add code to convert SVG code to HTML5 Canvas directly on your website by following the instructions at https://github.com/gabelerner/canvg.

Dale Stubbart

Fonts and Special Characters for Websites

Appendix A – Word to Text VBA Macro

If you have the full version of Microsoft Word, you can use this macro to change something typed in Word into HTML. Or, you can record your own VBA macro.

This macro changes fancy single quotes (`Chr(146)` and `Chr(147)`) to `&lsquo;` and `&rsquo;`. It changes hyphens and n-dashes to `&ndash;`.

It changes italics and bold to `<i>` and `<b>` tags.

It assumes your `<p>` tags are indented and that you've set up a class called `.indent` to indent lines within your `<p>` block as follows:

`<p>`This is the first sentence of this paragraph. Now I want a line break.`<br />`

`<span class="indent"></span>`This is the second line of the paragraph.`<br />`

`<span class="indent"></span>`This is the third line of the paragraph.

Dale Stubbart

Fonts and Special Characters for Websites

```
</p>
```
The CSS is as follows:
```
p {
text-indent: 1em;
}

.indent {
padding-left: 1em;
}
```

ToHtml macro:
```
Sub ToHtml()


  ' Capture current option for replacing quotes with fancy
quotes
  ' Turn this feature off
  ' start the HTML off as a paragraph
    sFormat =
Options.AutoFormatAsYouTypeReplaceQuotes
    Options.AutoFormatAsYouTypeReplaceQuotes =
False
    Selection.HomeKey Unit:=wdStory
    Selection.TypeText Text:="<p>"


  ' Replace special characters with HTML entities
    Selection.Find.ClearFormatting
    Selection.Find.Replacement.ClearFormatting
    With Selection.Find
      .Text = Chr(146)
      .Replacement.Text = "&rsquo;"
```

Dale Stubbart

Fonts and Special Characters for Websites

```
    .Forward = True
    .Wrap = wdFindContinue
    .Format = False
    .MatchCase = False
    .MatchWholeWord = False
    .MatchWildcards = False
    .MatchSoundsLike = False
    .MatchAllWordForms = False
End With
Selection.Find.Execute Replace:=wdReplaceAll
With Selection.Find
    .Text = Chr(145)
    .Replacement.Text = "&lsquo;"
    .Forward = True
    .Wrap = wdFindContinue
    .Format = False
    .MatchCase = False
    .MatchWholeWord = False
    .MatchWildcards = False
    .MatchSoundsLike = False
    .MatchAllWordForms = False
End With
Selection.Find.Execute Replace:=wdReplaceAll
With Selection.Find
    .Text = Chr(148)
    .Replacement.Text = "&rdquo;"
    .Forward = True
    .Wrap = wdFindContinue
    .Format = False
    .MatchCase = False
    .MatchWholeWord = False
```

Dale Stubbart

Fonts and Special Characters for Websites

```
    .MatchWildcards = False
    .MatchSoundsLike = False
    .MatchAllWordForms = False
End With
Selection.Find.Execute Replace:=wdReplaceAll
With Selection.Find
  .Text = Chr(147)
  .Replacement.Text = "&ldquo;"
  .Forward = True
  .Wrap = wdFindContinue
  .Format = False
  .MatchCase = False
  .MatchWholeWord = False
  .MatchWildcards = False
  .MatchSoundsLike = False
  .MatchAllWordForms = False
End With
Selection.Find.Execute Replace:=wdReplaceAll
With Selection.Find
  .Text = " - "
  .Replacement.Text = "&ndash;"
  .Forward = True
  .Wrap = wdFindContinue
  .Format = False
  .MatchCase = False
  .MatchWholeWord = False
  .MatchWildcards = False
  .MatchSoundsLike = False
  .MatchAllWordForms = False
End With
Selection.Find.Execute Replace:=wdReplaceAll
```

Dale Stubbart

Fonts and Special Characters for Websites

```
With Selection.Find
    .Text = Chr(151)
    .Replacement.Text = "&ndash;"
    .Forward = True
    .Wrap = wdFindContinue
    .Format = False
    .MatchCase = False
    .MatchWholeWord = False
    .MatchWildcards = False
    .MatchSoundsLike = False
    .MatchAllWordForms = False
End With
' Ellipsis
    Selection.Find.Execute Replace:=wdReplaceAll
    With Selection.Find
    .Text = Chr(133)
    .Replacement.Text = "&hellip;"
    .Forward = True
    .Wrap = wdFindContinue
    .Format = False
    .MatchCase = False
    .MatchWholeWord = False
    .MatchWildcards = False
    .MatchSoundsLike = False
    .MatchAllWordForms = False
End With

' Start each new line with an indent
    Selection.Find.Execute Replace:=wdReplaceAll
    With Selection.Find
    .Text = "^p"
```

Dale Stubbart

Fonts and Special Characters for Websites

```
        .Replacement.Text = "<br />^p<span
class=""indent""></span>"
        .Forward = True
        .Wrap = wdFindContinue
        .Format = False
        .MatchCase = False
        .MatchWholeWord = False
        .MatchWildcards = False
        .MatchSoundsLike = False
        .MatchAllWordForms = False
    End With
    Selection.Find.Execute Replace:=wdReplaceAll


  ' End with a closing paragraph tag
    Selection.EndKey Unit:=wdStory
    Selection.TypeText Text:="</p>"


  ' Change double line breaks to paragraph breaks
    Selection.Find.ClearFormatting
    Selection.Find.Replacement.ClearFormatting
    With Selection.Find
        .Text = "<br />^p<span
class=""indent""></span><br />"
        .Replacement.Text = "</p>^p"
        .Forward = True
        .Wrap = wdFindContinue
        .Format = False
        .MatchCase = False
        .MatchWholeWord = False
        .MatchWildcards = False
        .MatchSoundsLike = False
```

Dale Stubbart

```
        .MatchAllWordForms = False
    End With
    Selection.Find.Execute Replace:=wdReplaceAll
    With Selection.Find
        .Text = "</p>^p^p<span class=""indent""></span>"
        .Replacement.Text = "</p>^p^p<p>"
        .Forward = True
        .Wrap = wdFindContinue
        .Format = False
        .MatchCase = False
        .MatchWholeWord = False
        .MatchWildcards = False
        .MatchSoundsLike = False
        .MatchAllWordForms = False
    End With
    Selection.Find.Execute Replace:=wdReplaceAll

' Change italic, bold formatting to HTML
    Selection.Find.ClearFormatting
    Selection.Find.Font.Italic = True
    Selection.Find.Replacement.ClearFormatting
    With Selection.Find
        .Text = ""
        .Replacement.Text = "<i>^&</i>"
        .Forward = True
        .Wrap = wdFindContinue
        .Format = True
        .MatchCase = False
        .MatchWholeWord = False
        .MatchWildcards = False
        .MatchSoundsLike = False
```

Dale Stubbart

Fonts and Special Characters for Websites

```
        .MatchAllWordForms = False
End With
Selection.Find.Execute Replace:=wdReplaceAll
Selection.Find.ClearFormatting
Selection.Find.Font.Bold = True
Selection.Find.Replacement.ClearFormatting
With Selection.Find
   .Text = ""
   .Replacement.Text = "<b>^&</b>"
   .Forward = True
   .Wrap = wdFindContinue
   .Format = True
   .MatchCase = False
   .MatchWholeWord = False
   .MatchWildcards = False
   .MatchSoundsLike = False
   .MatchAllWordForms = False
End With
Selection.Find.Execute Replace:=wdReplaceAll


' Reset stuff
   Selection.Find.ClearFormatting
   Selection.Find.Replacement.ClearFormatting

   Options.AutoFormatAsYouTypeReplaceQuotes =
sFormat

   End Sub
```

Dale Stubbart

Fonts and Special Characters for Websites

About the Author

Dale Stubbart has worked with Computers for over 40 years. My Computer Consulting services include Websites. I also offer computer training. I do research, often quickly finding what others can't find or at least what they can't find quickly. You can find more information about my Computer Consulting Services at http://stubbart.com.

I have written several other computer books. I've also written Romance, Children's, SciFi, and books of other genres. You can find all of my books on my website.

Dale Stubbart

www.ingramcontent.com/pod-product-compliance
Lightning Source LLC
Chambersburg PA
CBHW051115050326
40690CB00006B/793